A Gift
from
Mrs. Wolfe

A PUPPY'S LIFE

A Gift
from
Mrs. Wolfe

by Sage Baldwin
and
Rita M. Wolfe

PHOTOS BY RITA M. WOLFE

MAXIMUS
PUBLISHING

A Puppy's Life

Published in the United States by Maximus Publishing

Permission requests should be mailed to: Maximus Publishing, Box 4455, Whitefish, Montana 59937

Publishers Cataloging-In-Publication Data
Baldwin, Sage and Rita M. Wolfe
A Puppy's Life / Sage Baldwin and Rita M. Wolfe
p. cm.
Contents—Dogs—Puppies—Growing up—Watch dogs grow.
Includes bibliographical references and index.
ISBN-10: 0-9792439-9-8
ISBN-13: 978-0-9792439-9-8
Summary: Full-color photographs and text highlight the growth and development of a Miniature Schnauzer puppy during the first two months of life.
1. Miniature schnauzers—Juvenile literature. 2. Puppies—Juvenile literature.
3. Dogs—Juvenile literature.
4. Parental behavior in animals—Juvenile literature.
[1. Dogs. 2. Animals—Infancy. 3. Parental behavior in animals.]
I. Title.
636.7'07-dc22
Library of Congress Control Number: 2007900032

Edited by Kitty Dowaliby
Photography by Rita M. Wolfe
Cover and interior design by Creative Expressions ETC

Printed in the United States of America

Table of Contents

My Life With Miniature Schnauzers

My name is Sage. I am ten years old and I grew up with Miniature Schnauzers. I will begin my story by sharing pictures of me and my dog family as I was growing up. Below are the Schnauzers owned by my grandparents. I will also introduce you to Barney and Elsa, my Schnauzers. Later I will show you some changes that take place in a puppy from birth to two months.

These are the special dogs who live with my grandma and grandpa. The dogs pictured from left to right are Babe, Fate, Maggie and Chelsie. Fate is the oldest of the dogs and the mother of Babe, Maggie and Chelsie. The dogs are groomed every few months so they look nice.

This is Grandpa and me when I was two years old. Maggie was one week old. She was the first puppy I saw.

This is Maggie, her brother and sisters at two weeks old. Puppies love to cuddle each other.

2

Fate is watching over Maggie, as a puppy. Over the years, Fate had three litters of puppies. Grandma kept one puppy out of each litter. The three dogs that my grandma kept are Chelsie, Babe and Maggie. Maggie is the youngest of the girls.

As I was growing up, the dogs often sat near me or followed me around the house. They loved the attention and affection I gave them.

I spoiled them with tasty dog biscuits. Maybe that was why they were always by my side.

We have gone camping in the great outdoors since I was little. The dogs love to camp and especially enjoy sleeping in the camper with me after a day in the woods.

Barney is my oldest Miniature Schnauzer. My parents purchased him when I was four years old. He is a wonderful dog for our family. Barney is a "people" dog. He loves grandma and grandpa's visits because they bring Maggie and her family.

Elsa is my other Miniature Schnauzer. My family loves having Elsa around. I enjoy the dogs and they have taught me to be a responsible person. Everyday, I must give them clean water, food and exercise. This keeps them strong and healthy.

Dogs need lots of love and attention. They need to be taken outdoors to get fresh air and to go potty several times a day. The dogs need baths and to be brushed at least weekly. They need to see the animal doctor every year for checkups and need to be given shots.

Breeding Takes Place

When I was nine years old, my grandpa and grandma bred Maggie so she could have a litter of puppies. It takes two months for an adult female dog to have a litter. This is called the gestation period.

Maggie proudly shows off her black and silver coloring. She has wonderful traits and my grandparents wanted to pass these traits on by breeding her.

This is Bunt, a male salt and pepper Miniature Schnauzer. Bunt is owned by another family who raises puppies and sells them. Bunt is used for breeding. They also make available other male dogs for breeding services. These people are known as breeders. Since breeders need to make money to stay in business, they charge a fee for the service they provide for others. Sometimes, the breeder prefers the pick of the litter instead of charging a fee.

8

Bunt was made available to Maggie for mating so she could have a litter of puppies. If the breeding is successful, Bunt and Maggie will become proud parents to a litter of puppies. The breeder wanted the pick of Maggie's puppies in exchange for the breeding fee.

To care for newborn puppies, you must prepare. Grandpa begins by making a whelping box. This is where the puppies will be born or whelped. The box should have a wooden floor. The sides of the box should be about one foot high. Grandpa puts hinges on one side of the box for easy cleaning. Guard rails must be built around the

inside of the box to prevent the mother from rolling over onto the pups and hurting them after they are born.

Maggie is inside the whelping box. The expectant mother should be allowed to sleep or spend time in the whelping box before the puppies are born. By doing so, she knows this is the location in which to have her pups.

A Puppy is Born, His Early Life

Two months later, Maggie became the proud mother of one male puppy. Usually, female dogs have more than one puppy. The puppy, named Max, was born at the veterinarian's clinic. Maggie was taken to the veterinarian's clinic because there was only one puppy inside of her and the puppy was too big to be born without the help of the veterinarian.

The veterinarian is holding Maggie and the newborn puppy. Max is only a few hours old. When puppies are born, they cannot see or hear and they do not have teeth.

Max is next to the soup can at one day old. This shows his size.

Max sleeps most of the time. He wakes up often to drink milk from his mother. When Max's tummy is full, he goes back to sleep.

Grandpa enjoys
holding Max while
he is sleeping at one
day old.

This is Max
when he is
four days old.
He is sleeping
in Grandpa's
hands.

Look closely! Can you see Maggie and Max snuggling together?

Here is another view of mom and her son relaxing and enjoying each other. Maggie is a wonderful mother to Max. She is very protective of her little one.

14

Miniature Schnauzer puppies need to visit the veterinarian when they are between three and five days old to get their tails docked. When puppies get their tails docked, it means the veterinarian shortens the length of the tail. Docking tails is a personal choice for Miniature Schnauzer owners.

It is also a good idea to get the puppy's dewclaws removed. Dewclaws are higher up on the leg, usually fastened by loose tissue. If left in place, the dewclaws could get caught on different surfaces and cause injury to the dog.

Max is five days old with his shortened tail. The other dogs are curious about Max's new appearance when he arrives back home from the veterinarian's clinic.

Max snuggles in a blanket at eight days old.

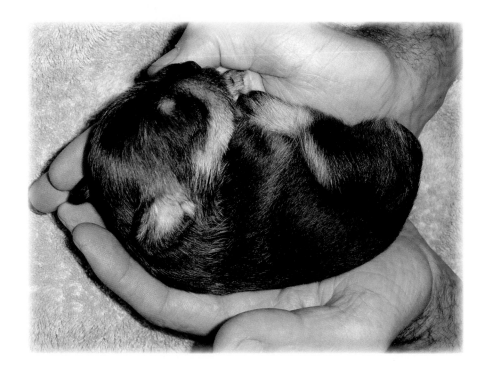

Miniature Schnauzer puppies are cute and cuddly.

16

Max is twelve days old when he opens his eyes for the first time. This is normal for puppies. When puppies finally open their eyes, the eye color is bluish gray. They are blind for several days but eventually will be able to see clearly at one month.

Max is growing up fast. Now he is bigger than the can at two weeks old.

YUMMY SOUP

This is a chart showing Max's weight during his first month of life. He gained about one ounce each day.

Max's Weight the First Month of Life	
Age	Weight
Day of birth	6 ounces
4 days old	8 ounces
6 days old	9 ounces
7 days old	10 ounces
8 days old	11 ounces
9 days old	12 ounces
10 days old	13 ounces
11 days old	14 ounces
12 days old	15 ounces
13 days old	16 ounces
14 days old (2 weeks old)	17 ounces
21 days old (3 weeks old)	1.8 pounds

Max's coat or hair is getting longer. He is still able to fit in Grandpa's hands at three weeks old.

Max starts to get his teeth and eat puppy food at four weeks old.

We begin housetraining Max at five weeks. This is his first day going potty outdoors.

Max is so adorable! He knows his name and will come running when he is called. Max likes chewing on shoes but if we tell him "no," he stops because he is such a smart puppy. Max loves to play with the dog toys in his home. We play with Max and exercise him regularly so he stays healthy.

Maggie and her son share the spotlight. Many changes have taken place during Max's first month of life.

Puppy Development & Socialization Timeline	
7-14 days old	Able to crawl
12-15 days old	Eyes begin to open
14-17 days old	Ears start to open
14-28 days old	Teeth begin to grow
16 days old	Able to walk
21 days old	Has normal gait
28 days old	Play-fights with others
28 days old	Hears and sees clearly

Max Touches Many Lives

Max is curious about the first snow fall at five weeks old. He sniffs the snow.

I share time with Max and my brother Logan. We take turns holding Max.

My mom holds Max at six weeks old. During this week, Max is being weaned from his mother. This means Max will no longer rely on his mother for milk. He eats mostly puppy food. Puppies need to be fed four times a day.

Max is more playful now
and loves to be held
and touched by people.

Logan gets his time
with the puppy. Many
people spoil Max.

Max is six weeks old. Maggie and her son love to play in the snow.

Max poses for the camera with his new toy. He knows exactly what to do when his picture gets taken. Max no longer chews on shoes. He chews on his toys instead.

Max starts to go up and down the stairs to go potty outdoors at seven weeks. He is now housetrained. Max loves to play with the other dogs and is the center of attention.

Max is almost too big for Grandpa's hands. He loves to be held by others. We want Max to be a "people" dog like Barney and the other dogs in our family.

At eight weeks old, Max visits the veterinarian. He is weighed, examined, and given the first of his puppy shots. Max has gained a lot of weight since his last visit to the veterinarian. He is in excellent health and weighs 3½ pounds. Max will be seeing the veterinarian at twelve weeks to continue his puppy shots. He will be seen at least one time per year to get his annual checkup and shots.

We are lucky to have Max. He was the only puppy born in this litter and the breeder had originally wanted the pick of the litter. She was kind enough to allow Grandma to keep the puppy. He will remain with us and be part of our loving Schnauzer family.

For eight years I have lived with Miniature Schnauzers. Grandma and Grandpa have raised this breed for twenty-five years. My entire family loves these dogs. Max is special to me and I will enjoy watching him grow.

American Kennel Club

If you are interested in AKC dog shows or "conformation" events showcasing your purebred dog, he or she must be registered with the American Kennel Club (AKC). At a conformation show, dogs are judged against their written breed standard. Besides conformation events there are obedience and performance events where all dogs can compete as athletes, regardless of breed.

When a litter is born, the owner of the litter must complete an AKC Litter Application and pay a litter fee if they want the puppies to be registered. After the AKC approves the Litter Application, they will send the litter owner an AKC Dog Registration Application for each puppy born in the litter. When the puppies are sold, the new owner will receive an AKC Dog Registration Application from the seller. The new owner must return the completed application and the required fee to the AKC if they want their puppy to be registered.

Our family followed the AKC procedures. Max will soon be registered, as are all the dogs that live at my grandparent's house. My dogs, Barney and Elsa, are also registered through the American Kennel Club.

More information about the American Kennel Club can be found at:

- American Kennel Club
- 5580 Centerview Drive
- Raleigh, NC 27606-3390
- (919) 233-9767
- www.akc.org

Glossary

Adult—an animal that is able to mate.

Breed—to produce young by mating.

Breeder—a person who raises animals mainly for breeding purposes.

Breeding Fee—the charge for the service of a male animal for breeding.

Coat—a natural outer covering, such as the hair or fur of an animal.

Dewclaws—claws higher up on the leg, usually fastened by loose tissue.

Dock—the part of an animal's tail after it has been shortened.

Gait—the manner or style of movement.

Gestation—the time between mating and giving birth.

Groom—to clean and maintain the appearance, such as the dog's coat.

Housetrain—to train an animal to be clean inside the house; to have the animal go potty outdoors.

Litter—a group of puppies born at the same time to the same mother; dogs usually have litters of four to six puppies.

Mammal—a warm-blooded animal that has a backbone; most mammals have hair or fur.

Mate—to join together to produce young.

Miniature Schnauzer—a breed of dog; a dog that originated in Germany and are characterized by a wiry coat, long head, pointed ears, heavy eyebrows, and long hair on the muzzle.

Muzzle—the jaws and nose of an animal.

Trait—a particular characteristic that can produce a type of behavior or condition; traits may be physical, such as hair color, or they may be behavioral, such as a dog's temperament.

Veterinarian—a medical doctor who treats animals.

Weaned—to take nourishment other than the mother's milk.

Whelp—the young offspring of a mammal.

Whelped—to give birth to a whelp or litter.

Index